From under the Bushel

From under the Bushel

A Guided Introduction to Meditative Prayer

LINDA L. GREENE

FROM UNDER THE BUSHEL
A GUIDED INTRODUCTION TO MEDITATIVE PRAYER

The views expressed in this work are solely those of the author and do not necessarily reflect the views of the publisher, and the publisher hereby disclaims any responsibility for them.

iUniverse books may be ordered through booksellers or by contacting:

iUniverse
1663 Liberty Drive
Bloomington, IN 47403
www.iuniverse.com
1-800-Authors (1-800-288-4677)

Because of the dynamic nature of the Internet, any web addresses or links contained in this book may have changed since publication and may no longer be valid. The views expressed in this work are solely those of the author and do not necessarily reflect the views of the publisher, and the publisher hereby disclaims any responsibility for them.

Any people depicted in stock imagery provided by Thinkstock are models, and such images are being used for illustrative purposes only.
Certain stock imagery © Thinkstock.

ISBN: 978-1-5320-4130-3 (sc)
ISBN: 978-1-5320-4131-0 (e)

Library of Congress Control Number: 2018900745

Print information available on the last page.

iUniverse rev. date: 01/22/2018

All scriptural quotations are taken from the
King James Version of the Bible.

To Judy, who makes me proud every day to be her "little thither." No one has ever known a better person or had a better friend.

Acknowledgments

I WANT TO thank the Reverend Lee Alison Crawford for helping me find myself as a Christian and for baptizing me two days before my sixty-third birthday. In addition, I'll always be grateful to you for taking some of my earlier prayers to the Holy Land with you and placing them in crevices in the Wailing Wall, as a dedication to my husband's deceased Jewish parents. Later on, you understood—and were not really surprised by—my unshakable need to become Roman Catholic.

In addition, I want to thank my dear friend Nancy, who always offers me moral support and true friendship. You may not know how much courage you provided for me to come out from under the bushel. When you, a non-Christian, read and liked the prayers and meditations, you gave me hope that this book might not only be preaching to the choir.

Why This Book

NEITHER DO MEN light a candle, and put it under a bushel, but on a candlestick; and it giveth light unto all that are in the house. Let your light so shine before men, that they may see your good works, and glorify your Father which is in heaven.

—Matthew 5:15–16

With this book, I am venturing from under the bushel. I am making public some prayers and meditations that I wrote over the past several years. Equally, I am making public some of my most personal feelings about meditation and about God.

Meditation, or meditative prayer, can seem like a huge and rather frightening task. After all, it is a practice most often associated with the great saints.

But you do not need to be a great saint to create prayers and meditations that deepen your own faith and move other people's hearts.

You need only dare to listen to your thoughts, feelings, questions, and answers. Find your voice, and step out from under the bushel.

I use the words "meditate" and "meditation" frequently in this book. Let's start, then, by defining what I mean when I use them.

First, you need to know what I do *not* mean. *I do not mean the practice of Eastern religions whose purpose is to empty the mind.*

Your mind will be very full indeed when you meditate, as I define it.

Saints and popes have written about meditation. You can find definitions and descriptions that make the process sound impossibly lofty and over your head.

The way I define the word in this book is much more accessible. It is the way many ordinary dictionaries define it:

- thinking deeply
- ruminating
- imagining
- pondering
- being there

Is this good enough? Shouldn't meditation be something loftier and more difficult? Shouldn't it be an especially holy task performed by especially holy people?

Well, for some people, meditation can grow into fruitful hours of contemplating the mysteries of God. For such people, that is wonderful.

But remember that pondering—simply pondering—is where it starts.

In the Gospel of Luke, after the shepherds visit the newborn Christ, we see the following: "But Mary kept all these things, and pondered them in her heart" (Luke 2:19 KJV).

In this passage, and in many others, Mary was shown to be a great ponderer. And although she surely took it further than we ever can, she is a fine role model. You can ponder with the best. In doing so, you can feel a deeper sense of peace and a stronger closeness to God.

Where and When to Meditate

You MIGHT DO some of your most fruitful meditation as you sit in a chair, with a Bible on your lap. At least, the very beginnings of your meditation may happen here. You read a passage. It grabs you. You begin to think. You begin to imagine. You want to be there.

You probably do need solitude for your meditation. Or you need to be with a companion who honors your wish to be silent as you do some deep thinking or some writing.

If you are in a "Wait! I can't hear myself think!" situation, this is not the time or place, because hearing yourself think is precisely what you need to do.

Most likely, of course, you will not be able to stay in that comfortable chair in that quiet place. One way to make meditation a part of your life is to realize that it can be a "take it with you" activity.

Once the spark has been ignited by a Bible scene or passage, you can do some fine meditation while you're folding laundry, raking leaves, or taking your daily walk around the block. You might not want to do it while you're waiting to fall asleep at night; the energy of it is likely to keep you awake. Still, there are some thoughts that are worth staying awake for.

My Background

As is true for many people, my first experiences with the Bible were with the King James Version, from early childhood, mostly in Sunday school or church or inside Christmas cards.

Years later, while earning a PhD in English literature from the University of Arkansas, I was steeped in the religious mindset of the medieval era. Equally important, my Shakespearean study made the language of the King James Version fairly comfortable for me to read. Not driven crazy by trying to figure out the meanings of words, I could enjoy their beauty.

Still, who are we kidding? I don't walk around quoting Chaucer, and I don't meditate in perfect Shakespearean verse. That early language can be difficult.

I needed to read the Bible again—and again—in more modern, more accessible language. I decided to read twenty pages each day, and that took me through the whole Bible within three months.

Then I started the same process again with a different version of the Bible. This time, I didn't try to go from beginning to end. I just kept a check sheet of what I had done and what I had not. By the time I started on the third version, I was going beyond the twenty allotted pages because it was getting easier and I was getting involved. Dare I say that it was becoming rather fun?

Therefore, more reading followed. I quickly realized that by doing as little as twenty pages per day, you can read three entire

Bibles in a year. But why would anyone want to read more than one? Because a passage that made no impression on you in one translation may really click in another.

For example, the first time I read about Jesus touching and curing a leper, I was awed by the miracle of the cure. The second time, in another translation and after I had reread Leviticus, I realized that there were two miracles. One of them was the miraculous courage Jesus showed in touching a visibly sick person, when he could have cured him at a distance and by word alone. Leviticus makes it clear that touching the visibly imperfect was simply not acceptable. So there were two miracles that day: the touch and the cure. One almost wonders which miracle seemed more amazing to the leper.

So I urge you: Read favorite passages here and there, again and again in this Bible and that. Revisit favorite stories and scenes. And just try to be there.

How to Use This Book

<hr />

THIS BOOK HAS two parts:

- Part 1 is made up of fifteen prayers and meditations of my own, followed by some of the Bible verses, ponderings, and thought processes that went into creating those fifteen. These are, in turn, followed by an area for you to express your own thoughts.
- Part 2 provides scenarios and questions to spark your own meditations, as well as a space for your notes toward creating them.

My hope is that you will not only enjoy the readings in the first part of the book but that they will indeed spark some of your own ideas. Then I hope that you decide to meditate in response to the ideas presented in part 2.

Part 1

My Prayers and Meditations

THERE IS A progress in my prayers and meditations as they are arranged in this book. The earliest ones, though somewhat related to Bible passages that I especially like, do not ponder actual Bible scenes or ask questions about those scenes.

They relate more to personal questions I had about my own faith and its development and what it meant to me:

- Was faith available to me?
- Where was it, and where did it come from?
- What did it feel like?

Later, I began to think more about specific Bible scenes or people and to build meditations upon those.

Your own progress into meditation may be very different. Honor it, follow it, and see where it takes you. In the final section of this book, I'll show you several approaches that will help you get started.

Behind the Walls

"Let there be light," you said,
And with the breath of pure creativity,
You began to make the light.
"Let there be light," I whispered,
And with the breath of pure mercy,
You began to show me what you had made.
Trembling, I asked,
"Where has this light been all these years?"
Smiling, you replied,
"Behind your private walls.
You only needed to dare look for it."

On "Behind the Walls"

And God said, Let there be light: and there was light.
—Genesis 1:3 KJV

THE WORDS "LET there be light" can have very different meanings, depending upon how they are spoken and by whom.

In the mouth of God, they are a strong, creative imperative. He speaks—or thinks—and his will is done.

In the mouth of an ordinary person, the same words can be curious or eager or desperate. They can be timid or demanding. They can be as many things as there are people to say them.

When I was pondering these words, I thought about the pain of people suffering depression or grief, sometimes for a lifetime. For them, there may seem to be no light.

This meditation became a dialogue between an all-powerful creator and a hesitant, frightened person who needed light and who half-doubted that it could ever appear.

Taking the first step of courage, the person asks for light and discovers that God has been ready to make it available all along. It was the person's fears and walls that stood in the way.

Your Thoughts

_____
_____
_____
_____
_____
_____
_____
_____

Where Faith Lives

Somewhere in my bones, oh Lord,
The arguments about politics and society
Begin to diminish.
Somewhere in my bones, oh Lord,
The debates about science and divinity
Begin to ebb.
Somewhere in my bones, oh Lord,
My fears and doubts
Release their hold on me.
Somewhere, deep in my bones,
I whisper, "Yes,"
Become silent,
And adore you.

On "Where Faith Lives"

This is what the Sovereign Lord says to these bones: I will make breath[a] enter you, and you will come to life. I will attach tendons to you and make flesh come upon you and cover you with skin; I will put breath in you, and you will come to life. Then you will know that I am the Lord.
—Ezekiel 37:5–6 KJV

THE ABOVE PASSAGE is a small portion of an Old Testament story known as the Valley of Dry Bones.

I do not know whether the passage was the conscious inspiration for "Where Faith Lives." I do know that, at this point in my life, there is a kind of interplay between them. When I read the Valley of Dry Bones, I think of my meditation. When I read my meditation, I think of the Valley of Dry Bones.

It seems like a reasonable connection. When faith enters someone and makes them "know that I am the Lord," it puts breath into them and makes them "come to life."

YOUR THOUGHTS

_____
_____
_____
_____
_____
_____

Memories of a Dream from Childhood

Come, Jesus.
Put your hand on my shoulder,
And we will walk together across the lawn.
And I,
Not yet worthy to see your full glory,
Will look at our shadows in the grass
And smile.

On "Memories of a Dream from Childhood"

PERHAPS YOU'VE HAD a dream like this. It may not have the same plot line, but it is likely a dream that has both comforted you and haunted you for many years.

I had no idea who my shadow companion was in this dream. Then I realized that since the companion was not already defined and specific (i.e., it was not a relative or a specific friend), I could choose who it should be.

When I got older, I quietly slipped into a decision that the shadows were of Jesus and me, walking together.

It felt right. It still does. And I think about that dream when I need to walk with him.

YOUR THOUGHTS

A Statement of Faith

Not because I understand.
I don't.
Not because I comprehend.
I can't.
But deliberately,
As an act of free will,
As a statement of choice,
Only and entirely
Because you said so,
I believe.

On "A Statement of Faith"

When Jesus came into the coasts of Caesarea
Philippi, he asked his disciples, saying, Whom do
men say that I the Son of man am? And they said,
Some say that thou art John the Baptist: some, Elias;
and others, Jeremias, or one of the prophets.
He saith unto them, But whom say ye that I
am? And Simon Peter answered and said, Thou
art the Christ, the Son of the living God.
—Matthew 16:13–16 KJV

THE FIRST TIME I read Peter's confession of faith, I was dazzled
by his quiet certainty. I had always wanted that kind of faith.
Somehow, though, I felt that such faith had to be preceded by
a huge event, or that it had to be accompanied by a massive
emotion.

As a shy person, "huge" and "massive" didn't work too well
for me.

Then I heard a priest on television talking about how faith
is not a feeling; it is a decision. Wait! You mean I could just
decide? An ordinary person like me?

Yes, it turns out that I could. I merely had to make a decision
and a commitment. And once that commitment was made, I
could protect it as a spouse protects their marital commitment.

I did not need to test my faith by reading material that
contradicted Christianity, any more than I needed to test my

marital commitment by dating other men. I did not need to listen to skeptics putting down Christianity. I did not need to reask myself, "Why do I believe?"

I could just repeat to myself my own commitment and my own words, "Because you said so." And perhaps I would reread Peter's words too.

YOUR THOUGHTS

_____

_____

_____

_____

_____

_____

_____

Morning Meditation

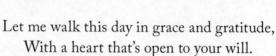

Let me walk this day in grace and gratitude,
With a heart that's open to your will.
Lead me one step closer to an understanding
Of your love and my purpose.
Keep me ever mindful
Of the magnitude of your suffering
When I am tempted to complain of my own.
Give me strength, courage, kindness, and faith.
My Lord, make me worthy.

On "Morning Meditation"

⸻

O God, thou art my God; early will I seek thee:
my soul thirsteth for thee, my flesh longeth for thee
in a dry and thirsty land, where no water is.
—Psalm 63:1 KJV

I LOVE MORNING prayers. Although we haven't actually been without God all night, it may feel as though we have. Therefore, we can feel a hunger to reestablish the connection.

Although there are hundreds of wonderful morning prayers, I wanted to write my own too. This one came, as though written in the hidden layers of my brain, when I wasn't trying.

Perhaps, then, "meditation" is not the correct description for it, since there was no pondering or effort involved. For me, the words summed up my most heartfelt wishes for each day.

You have your own personal morning meditation, whether or not it has found words yet. You start the day with things you want—for your heart, for your mind, for your friends, and for the world. These make up your meditation. When they are ready to find words, they will.

Linda L. Greene

Your Thoughts

_____

_____

_____

_____

_____

_____

_____

A Singer's Prayer

Grant me my voice for your praise,
Not mine, not mine.
Grant me my strength for your will,
Not mine, not mine.
Holding my hand in yours, gently you lead me,
Keeping me safe when I'm lost on my way.
Walking beside me, Lord, hourly you teach me
Doubt and despair shall be not mine.

On "A Singer's Prayer"

And when thou prayest, thou shalt not be as the hypocrites
are: for they love to pray standing in the synagogues and
in the corners of the streets, that they may be seen of
men. Verily I say unto you, They have their reward.
—Matthew 6:5 KJV

But all their works they do for to be seen of
men: they make broad their phylacteries, and
enlarge the borders of their garments ...
—Matthew 23:5 KVJ

As a child, when I created something, I always urged people,
excitedly, "See what I did. Hear what I sang. Taste what I
made." Perhaps this is the universal way of children.

When I first read the above two readings from Matthew,
I was reminded that the need to be set apart, to be looked at,
and to be admired is less charming in adults.

Certainly, we are allowed to be pleased with our successes.
But if we did the work, in the first place, only to be admired,
then there is a problem.

We must remember that our talents and our successes are a
gift from God. In our hearts, we should give him credit. This
meditation is a reminder to myself of that fact.

16

Your Thoughts

_____
_____
_____
_____
_____
_____
_____
_____

A Prayer for Calmness

My Lord and my God,
Come calm the roiling waters of my mind,
That I may feel you in the stillness.
Soften my voice,
That I may hear yours above me.
Slow my hurried steps,
That I may linger beside you
And learn your ways.

On "A Prayer for Calmness"

And when he was entered into a ship, his disciples
followed him. And, behold, there arose a great
tempest in the sea, insomuch that the ship was
covered with the waves: but he was asleep.
And his disciples came to him, and awoke him, saying,
Lord, save us: we perish. And he saith unto them, Why are
ye fearful, O ye of little faith? Then he arose, and rebuked
the winds and the sea; and there was a great calm.
—Matthew 8:23–26 KJV

I WAS GOING through a complicated time when I wrote this prayer. Both of my parents had just died, within a couple of months of each other, and now I was facing health concerns for my husband too.

My emotions became a stormy sea. At such times, I talk too loudly, walk too quickly, and worry too much.

One morning, the Mass reading was about Jesus calming the sea. Not only did he calm the sea, but he willingly woke up out of a much-needed nap and calmed that unruly sea for a bunch of cranky disciples who were scared, whiny, and not very faithful at that moment.

I decided to ask him to calm my own storms as well. He did, both on this occasion and many other times when I prayed this prayer.

YOUR THOUGHTS

In a Seeming Absence

In the laughing and the stillness,
You are God.
In the singing and the stillness,
You are God.
In the weeping and the stillness,
You are God.
In the raging and the stillness,
You are God.
In the stillness that feels like absence,
You are God.

On "In a Seeming Absence"

And he said, Go forth, and stand upon the mount
before the Lord. And, behold, the Lord passed by,
and a great and strong wind rent the mountains,
and brake in pieces the rocks before the Lord; but
the Lord was not in the wind: and after the wind an
earthquake; but the Lord was not in the earthquake:
And after the earthquake a fire; but the Lord was not
in the fire: and after the fire a still small voice.
And it was so, when Elijah heard it, that he wrapped
his face in his mantle, and went out, and stood in the
entering in of the cave. And, behold, there came a voice
unto him, and said, What doest thou here, Elijah?
—1 Kings 19:11–13 KJV

Be still, and know that I am God.
—Psalm 46:10 KJV

IN BOTH OF the passages above, God manifested himself in a
still, small voice.

We often make assumptions about what God will look or
sound like when he is near us. We may expect earthquakes and
great and strong winds. In the absence of these, we may feel an
absence of God himself.

Similarly, we have ideas about the kinds of occasions where
God would deign to be near us. Perhaps, we think, he is not

there during laughter, because laughter isn't solemn. But, then, he created laughter, didn't he?

We may feel that he is not there when there is rage. Moses, though, expressed anger to God and was not deserted for it. Jesus himself expressed anger more than once, most notably when he drove the money changers from the temple.

If we expect to see God only in huge, somber, or "nice" things, we may miss his presence when we most need it.

Your Thoughts

_____
_____
_____
_____
_____
_____
_____

In an Arid Time

When you're feeling
Spiritual disconsolation,
Lift your voice up
Where your heart won't go.
And when you're feeling
Dark and empty desolation,
Still lift your voice up
Where your heart won't go.
Tell him you doubt him.
Tell him you're scared.
Tell him you don't always know he cares.
Tell him your heart is chilled and heavy.
Tell him you're not even sure he's there.
Just tell him.
Talk to him.
Even if you feel alone.
When your prayers seem arid
And devoid of feeling,
He still loves you,
More than you can ever know.
He can see the fragile faith that you are offering,
When you lift your voice up
Where your heart won't go.

On "In an Arid Time"

And the Lord shall guide thee continually, and
satisfy thy soul in drought, and make fat thy bones:
and thou shalt be like a watered garden, and like
a spring of water, whose waters fail not.
—Isaiah 58:11 KJV

I HAVE HEARD many of my friends from church talk about the pain of arid times in prayer. These are times when you don't seem to have the energy to pray. Or you cannot seem to come up with the right words.

Arid times come with no ready explanation for them, and they make prayer very difficult. Just remember that no one says you need to lift up your voice in your own original, brilliant language—only that you should lift it up. The Psalms, especially, are perfect for such times as these.

Psalm 22 is a wonderful old standby, moving as it does from misery to hope. The first two lines express the depths of your misery, despair, or dryness:

My God, my God, why hast thou forsaken
me? why art thou so far from helping me, and
from the words of my roaring? O my God, I cry
in the day time, but thou hearest not; and in the
night season, and am not silent.

Lines 11 through 14 describe your troubles and enemies:

> ... for trouble is near; for there is none to help. Many bulls have compassed me: strong bulls of Bashan have beset me round. They gaped upon me with their mouths, as a ravening and a roaring lion. I am poured out like water, and all my bones are out of joint: my heart is like wax; it is melted in the midst of my bowels.

Although modern woes probably have nothing to do with bulls and lions, the vivid imagery is perfectly valid for modern-day troubles: depression, fear, worry, sickness, rage, or dryness. God will understand you when you use these metaphors to express your pain.

Then, later on, Psalm 22 gives a ray of hope and makes clear that God is there after all:

> I will declare thy name unto my brethren: in the midst of the congregation will I praise thee. Ye that fear the Lord, praise him; all ye the seed of Jacob, glorify him; and fear him, all ye the seed of Israel. For he hath not despised nor abhorred the affliction of the afflicted; neither hath he hid his face from him; but when he cried unto him, he heard.

Sometimes I read Psalm 22 in my arid times. Other times, I sit beside the window, pet my cat, and go directly to a psalm of praise, even though I'm not feeling particularly praiseful at the moment. For this, I love Psalm 148 in its entirety.

Most often of all, I raise up my voice by going through the

entire set of psalms, stopping at favorite underlined passages and reading them aloud. Yes, aloud.

Does this change the fact that I feel dry and dull? Well, sometimes it actually does. When it doesn't, at least I'm spending my arid and difficult time talking to my best friend.

Your Thoughts

The Gifts from and to God

(5:00 a.m.)
You greet me and smile.
"Little one. I give you your day."
From your strong hands, I take the lumps of clay,
Heavy and wonderful,
Unformed, unshaped, unused.
In your quiet eyes, I read the unspoken request:
"Make me a gift."
I spend hours molding, shaping,
Reshaping when possible,
Working until the clay
can no longer be worked.
(10:00 p.m.)
I look at my creation, finished and formed,
The clay wholly used.
My gift, tiny and ordinary—the best I can do.
With childish pride and some regrets,
I tremble a bit, greet you, and blush.
Hesitantly extending my little gift, I say,
"God our Father, I offer you my day."

On "The Gifts from and to God"

GOD IS ALWAYS giving us gifts. The first is our very lives—and then, every morning, life again with all its possibilities. Some of the gifts we can see; some we cannot.

Many of us learn to accept the more intangible gifts from God. What we may not learn to accept is the fact that it's a two-way street. We really do give gifts back to him, and he recognizes them as such.

Certainly, there are few of us who can cure a disease, paint a deathless painting, or build a cathedral. But these are not the only kinds of gifts we can make out of the fresh clay of our day.

Gifts—and givers—do not need to be huge in order to be worth his smile.

- Perhaps the gift is a leading question to start a conversion with the guy who sweeps the floor in your restaurant—the guy who is usually ignored.
- Maybe the gift is to pay, secretly, for that table's Big Macs.
- Maybe it is to say something witty to someone who hasn't had a good laugh in days.
- Maybe it is to refrain from saying something witty and nasty to someone who's driving you nuts.

He does give us the clay. We can give him back our gifts and feel his smile.

Your Thoughts

_____

_____

_____

_____

_____

_____

_____

That Other Gethsemane

I wonder, were you scared that night,
That other Night Before?
Did you tremble and sweat blood
As you recognized what lay ahead?
Did you sink to your knees
As you foresaw the scourges
Of hate and disbelief
That awaited you?
Did you weep to anticipate
The thorns of betrayal
You would suffer?
Did you dread the long, long walk
To Calvary
With the sins of all the world
On your back?
And, with tears still drying on your face,
Did you whisper, "But I love them, Father.
Let our will begin,"
As you left his side
And softly entered
The waiting womb of your mother?

On "That Other Gethsemane"

⸻

And being in an agony he prayed more earnestly:
and his sweat was as it were great drops of
blood falling down to the ground.
—Luke 22:44 KJV

THREE OF THE Gospels describe Christ's hours in the Garden of Gethsemane, the night before his crucifixion. The above passage from Luke well serves as a summary of the level of agony Christ suffered.

That night before, Jesus knew what was going to happen and just how bad it was going to be.

I often remember that he knew all of this before his conception too. For him, to choose to be conceived at all was to choose to be tired and hungry, to suffer all manner of human woes, to feel frustrated, humiliated, and angry—and eventually to be tortured and executed.

The night before his incarnation, then, was another "night before," not entirely unlike the terrifying hours in Gethsemane. And yet he chose to come.

Your Thoughts

_____

_____

_____

_____

_____

_____

_____

Little Boy

Mother Mary, chosen by God,
Tell me things that only you
Could know.
Teach me about the eternal Word.
Teach me things about my Lord,
Your little boy.
In those quiet times of day
When you used to watch him play,
Did you ponder?
Did you wonder what he knew?
What he would say, what he could do?
And did you pray to know—or not to know?
When you helped him learn the words,
When you helped him say the names
Of things he saw,
Of all the things that he had made,
Did you teach him who his father was,
Or did he teach you?
Trying once to stand up tall
And be a big boy after all.
Then falling hard upon the ground
That was his own.
When did he know the world was his,
That he could use it as his toy,
If he were indeed that kind of boy?

When, instead, did he decide
To touch the untouchable, to love the unlovable,
To speak the unspeakable,
Calling "Abba" to his God,
While elders looked on him as odd and defiant?
Did you feel a flicker then?
Did a sword of worry touch your heart,
A mother's worry for her little boy
And Lord?

On "Little Boy"

And he went down with them, and came to
Nazareth, and was subject unto them: but his
mother kept all these sayings in her heart.
—Luke 2:51 KJV

WHATEVER ELSE JESUS was, he was once a little boy, part of a
family and "subject unto" his parents.

Some years ago, I read a book that presented an image that
blew me away. Unfortunately, I do not remember the name of
the book. Therefore, I cannot cite it properly and give credit to
its author.

The image was of Mary praying to God in heaven while
God played on the floor at her feet.

I was drawn by the amazing interplay between the daily
routine and the divinity that must have been ever present in
that family. For better or worse, even the most ordinary things
cannot be ordinary if your child is God.

No wonder his mother had things to keep in her heart and
ponder. It made me want to talk with her about her little boy.
This meditation barely taps the surface of the things we might
all want to ask this mother.

YOUR THOUGHTS

In the Mind of a Righteous Jew in the Crowd

HE WAS HERE again, that man Yeshua from Nazareth. And I went again to hear him, as I always do now, whenever he is within walking distance. I cannot seem to stay away.

He draws me.

And he terrifies me.

Each time my heart compels me to walk miles to sit in the crowd, I become nearly faint with fear when it is time to return home.

What will I find there?

My wife and children—will they still be alive? Will my house still stand?

For years, I have heard the scriptural stories of entire cities—thousands of people—struck down by our angry God.

Their sin was always the same, much like mine: being attracted by other gods.

This Yeshua claims to be equal to God sometimes, and I sit there and listen.

Will my own audacity lead to such a scenario—dead bodies piled in the street, being devoured by birds and wild animals?

It has happened before for such sins as mine. This I have known for years.

And yet he draws me.

I go to hear him. And now I have done so again.

Many times, I have listened with curiosity and even interest. But today was worse. I listened and felt my heart lighten with something resembling hope, or even love … until, with a jolt, I returned to my senses.

Now I must make a sin offering. I must close my ears and my eyes. I must be careful and good and righteous. I must stay away the next time this Yeshua comes near.

And yet he draws me.

God help me, he does draw me.

On "In the Mind of a Righteous Jew in the Crowd"

———◆———

And God spoke all these words: "I am the Lord your
God, who brought you out of Egypt, out of the land of
slavery. "You shall have no other gods before[a] me.
—Exodus 20:1–3 KJV

But if thine heart turn away, so that thou wilt not hear, but
shalt be drawn away, and worship other gods, and serve them;
I denounce unto you this day, that ye shall surely perish,
and that ye shall not prolong your days upon the land,
whither thou passest over Jordan to go to possess it.
—Deuteronomy 30:17–18 KJV

To ACCEPT GOD as the *only* God is the first of the Ten
Commandments.

As you read through the Old Testament, you see how defeat,
famine, plague, and exile—all manner of dreadful things—
followed Israelites who dared to turn their backs on God and
worship anyone or anything else.

How was the man in this meditation to know that Jesus
really was God and that the right thing to do was to follow him?

How did he know that his desire to hear Jesus wasn't
from the devil? How did he know he wasn't going to cause

cataclysms—for himself, for his loved ones, even for all Jews—by following his yearnings?

This man Yeshua hinted strongly that he himself was god. He dared insist that he had authority and could interpret, explain, and reinterpret sayings from the scriptures.

Do you ever wonder how you would have reacted if you had been there in the crowd, perhaps at the Sermon on the Mount?

You wouldn't have had the advantage of knowing how the story turned out. There would have been no resurrection yet to think about and to help you decide your feelings. There would have been no New Testament to read for guidance.

Jesus would have just been "that man Yeshua," "Jesus of Nazareth." Maybe you had actually seen a miracle or heard him speak. Maybe you had only heard about him, from people who feared him or hated him or were attracted to him.

You yourself might have been a deeply devout man, like Paul before his conversion. Like that early Paul, you might have been repelled by Yeshua as a danger and a disgrace.

Or you might have been more like the man in this meditation, drawn but confused and frightened by that insistent pull.

Your Thoughts

_____
_____
_____
_____
_____
_____
_____
_____

Thomas at Supper

───────────────◦∞◦───────────────

I REMEMBER WHEN he first talked about the body and the blood. People were horrified. Some were amused. Most were struck dumb. Many slipped away with the kind of nervous half glance that says, "I thought I knew him, but he's mad now. Was he always so?"

He asked us, then, if we too wanted to leave, and Peter led us in saying that we did not.

But I wonder, What if he had asked us to actually drink the blood that very day?

What would we have done? Would we have drunk bravely, for loyalty's sake, in the excitement of the moment? Then would we have somehow understood the strange new ritual as it unfurled?

Or would we have sipped tentatively, trying to control our convulsing throats, while wondering if we should have walked away after all.

And now it's here again, this talk about eating flesh and drinking blood.

And this time, it's more than talk.

A yearning invitation: "Do you love me enough?" it seems to say. "Do you believe?"

Do we?

One thing is certain: If we actually do this, we can't go back again. We will have made a choice between the unspeakable and the incomprehensible.

And nothing will ever be the same again.

On "Thomas at Supper"

———⪘———

> And whatsoever man there be of the house of Israel, or of the
> strangers that sojourn among you, that eateth any manner
> of blood; I will even set my face against that soul that eateth
> blood, and will cut him off from among his people ...
> Therefore I said unto the children of Israel, No
> soul of you shall eat blood, neither shall any
> stranger that sojourneth among you eat blood.
> —Leviticus 17:10 and 12 KJV

As PASSAGES IN the Old Testament indicate, the eating of blood
was anathema to the Jews—a law handed down for hundreds
of years.

In the Gospel of John (7:22–71), well before the Last
Supper, Jesus speaks at length about his being the bread of life.
He preaches the need for believers to eat his flesh and drink
his blood.

Note that he never softens this strange statement by
claiming that he doesn't mean it literally. Nor does he soften it
by explaining that blood and flesh can be miraculously hidden
under the more palatable appearances of wine and bread, once
he creates the new sacrament. He just puts it out there boldly:
his believers must eat his flesh and drink his blood, or they are
not really his believers.

People are shocked and revolted by Jesus's vivid words.

Many of his listeners decide that he is mad or blasphemous or both. It is a turning point; many run away that day.

But his twelve disciples (including Doubting Thomas) remain. Even they are not entirely comfortable with the idea, at that point. When asked if they are leaving too, Peter replies, "Lord, to whom shall we go? thou hast the words of eternal life" (John 6:68).

Although a statement of loyalty to Jesus, this is hardly a ringing endorsement of his words about blood and flesh.

What a huge decision the disciples had to make, later at the last supper. This was the sacrament and the test. It was all or nothing.

It couldn't have been easy. I wonder how I would have felt. Perhaps you do too.

Your Thoughts

_____

_____

_____

_____

_____

_____

_____

Pentecost

They say you come in fire, and so you do
For many.
So I wait for you to come
In flames that I can see —
Flames that will blind me
And make me see a new world instead.
Then I will know that you are there.
They say you come in tongues, and so you do
For many.
So I wait for you to come
In wild, strange words that I can hear —
Words that will reach me
And teach me to translate
A new world instead.
Then I will know that you are there.
But, for me, there is no fire;
There are no tongues.
And I wonder if I am alone.
Then I see a leaf touched by a breeze.
I hear my own voice whisper, "Oh."
I feel a gentle companion,
A soft gratitude,
And I know that I do not require
The fire.

On "Pentecost"

And when the day of Pentecost was fully come, they
were all with one accord in one place. And suddenly
there came a sound from heaven as of a rushing mighty
wind, and it filled all the house where they were sitting.
And there appeared unto them cloven tongues like as
of fire, and it sat upon each of them. And they were all
filled with the Holy Ghost, and began to speak with
other tongues, as the Spirit gave them utterance.
—Acts 2:1–4 KVJ

AT PENTECOST, IN the Acts of the Apostles, there are dramatic
manifestations of the descent of the Holy Spirit. Not only the
disciples but many others saw what happened that day. I've
always been a bit jealous of the people, like those in this scene
from Acts, who have such large and expansive experiences
of God.

The theme in this meditation is, again, that although God
can indeed visit in a spectacular theophany, he also can and
does visit in small ways and small things to ordinary people. It
is my comfort—and possibly yours.

YOUR THOUGHTS

_____

_____

_____

_____

_____

_____

_____

Part 2

Suggestions for Meditation

Creating Your Own Meditations

———— ❧ ————

THERE ARE A couple of important prerequisites for meditating, as described in this book:

- You have to want to do it.
- You have to recognize that it is something that you indeed can do.

There are four other guidelines:

- Let the topic choose you.
- Use the "if I were the one" technique.
- Look at the little things.
- Look behind the scenes.

LET THE TOPIC CHOOSE YOU

You may think, *I don't know what to meditate about.*

In a sense, you don't have to choose what to meditate on. It chooses you. Perhaps, right now, you're thinking, *But it's my choice to meditate on that passage that I read last week.* Well, yes. You're choosing it today. But really it chose you last week when it settled into your mind and wouldn't go away.

That's the key. When you are reading your Bible or listening to someone speak about faith, a passage pops out at you. It might even be just a couple of words. It will grab you and seem more important to you than all the other words around it. It will probably keep recurring to you.

Why? Some might say that God is trying to call your mind to something when this happens. The why isn't really important. It is not a matter of logic, nor is it meant to be. If those words or thoughts start knocking at your door, then, by definition, they are important. Go with them and find out where their importance lies. What might your thoughts turn into?

USE THE "IF I WERE THE ONE" TECHNIQUE

I remember reading Leviticus. A bunch of boring, ancient rules, right?

Then it hit me that if I were the person finding the pimple on my forehead, I'd really care about the rules pertaining to skin eruptions. If I were the person whose ox was wounded, I'd care about what kind of recompense there might be.

In short, if I were "the one," I'd care about a lot of the rules in Leviticus, since those things would determine what my life would be like in my society.

Let the words "if I were the one" become an insistent background to your thinking about faith and the Bible. They will always add a dimension.

LOOK AT THE LITTLE THINGS

Although, in a sense, the Bible is the biggest book in the world, every big thing in it is surrounded by many little ones.

I invite you to step inside the minds and bodies of the peripheral people in Bible scenes. Imagine the full range of their feelings. Everything they could feel, you can. Everything you can feel, they could.

Don't get caught up in the idea that every element in the Bible is lofty, or that all of its people are holy. The Bible is about God, but it is also, wonderfully and always, about plain old human beings.

In fact, that is where a lot of the drama comes in. Here are these ordinary people, like us, walking around in an eternity-changing series of events.

There were achy backs and grumbling stomachs in the crowds listening to Jesus. There were mundane financial worries. There were concerns about children and family. And often, there were miracles, small and big.

In doing the meditations in this chapter, you will have a chance, if you wish, to pay close attention to that interplay between the divine and the ordinary.

Look behind the Scenes

For everything that happens in the Bible, something happened before that scene. Something happened after it. Something was happening behind the scene while it was playing out.

It can be fun to imagine these "befores," "afters," and "behinds." You will have a chance here to do so. So let's begin.

Mary Getting Water

THERE ARE NO Bible scenes specifically about Mary getting water, but this is something that she would have done every day, with the rest of the women, in the cool of the morning.

It provides several themes for meditation.

ON THE MORNING AFTER THE ANNUNCIATION

As the women filled their jugs, they would have talked, both to ease the drudgery of the task and to be friendly.

For men in Nazareth, conversations were often about the scriptures and politics. One of the favorite topics was the Messiah, with speculation about what he would be like, where he would come from, what he could or would do.

For the women, much of the early-morning conversation at the well or river would have been about family matters: babies and husbands and household tasks. Perhaps there was even gossip, gentle or not so gentle, about neighbors.

Here, away from the men, the women may have also felt free to discuss scriptural and political matters themselves. They too could talk about the Messiah.

In this scenario, the women are speculating about the Messiah's mother.

- What will she be like?
- Who could possibly be worthy of such an honor?

- What would it be like to actually raise a child as important as the Messiah?
- What if you actually met her?

Meanwhile, unlike the rest of the women, Mary knows who the mother of the Messiah will be, because it is she.

She isn't supposed to divulge this fact, but what does she say? What does she think?

Your Thoughts

_____

_____

_____

_____

_____

_____

_____

Mary, Beginning to Show

RIGHT AFTER THE Annunciation, Mary left to visit her cousin Elizabeth, who was pregnant—at an advanced age—with the child who would be John the Baptist. She stayed with Elizabeth until the child was born. An older woman certainly needed all the help and support she could get.

Mary has been gone for three months. People talk.

Now she is back, and she looks pregnant to her savvy friends.

Take it from there. They don't know what we know about Mary. So what are they thinking?

- Mary is betrothed but not officially married. Did she choose not to wait? That wasn't entirely unacceptable in her era.
- She lives in a dangerous world where women away from home could be seduced or raped. Could something have happened?
- Was it hard for the women to talk at all, not knowing if the child was the result of love or horror? You can do some interesting pondering on what the women think, as well as what they say. What about their body language toward her?
- Does Mary talk about her cousin's miraculous old-age pregnancy? If so, does it get anyone thinking about the possibilities of other miracles surrounding pregnancy?

- Does anyone remember their earlier discussion of the Messiah's mother?

YOUR THOUGHTS

_____

_____

_____

_____

_____

_____

_____

Child Jesus in the Temple

THE GOSPEL OF Luke (3:41–52) tells of the twelve-year-old Jesus staying behind in Jerusalem when his family leaves for home after their Passover pilgrimage. This tiny scene offers many possibilities for meditation if you ponder not only the short story itself but the events that could have happened before and after it.

BEFORE THE BIBLE STORY

Before this biblical story takes place, the family and the townspeople are preparing themselves to go to Jerusalem for the Passover.

See, feel, and hear their excitement. Passover, after all, is a big deal and a welcome change from ordinary daily life.

Dare to imagine many possibilities before the Bible story even starts:

- Does Jesus have a different feeling about Passover this year? It was apparently either the last of his childhood or the first of his manhood.

- How does the child Jesus behave as the trip is getting started? Does he mingle with the children? Or, now twelve, does he spend more time with the adults, talking with them and helping them?

- Imagine that an old man in the crowd is very ill. This will surely be his last Passover. How does Jesus relate to this man? Maybe he talks to him much as he would later speak to the crowds. How does he comfort the man? Maybe the old man has a colorful way of talking, and he teaches the receptive and brilliant young Jesus how to tell stories.

Your Thoughts

_____

_____

_____

_____

_____

_____

_____

Inside the Actual Bible Scene

────────◆────────

You CAN ALSO look deeper inside the actual Bible story of the Finding in the Temple—inside people's minds while the event was playing out.

- Had he planned to stay behind? Or was it an impulse? Or was it just an accident?
- Is Jesus scared to be away from his family?
- Is Jesus nervous around these great teachers? Or is he steady and newly confident? In his mind, are the teachers going to teach him, or is he going to teach them?
- How do the teachers feel? Surely, it is nice to have a really good student. But perhaps there is one teacher who is a bit jealous that this child can outthink him. How does that play out?
- Could Joseph of Arimathea have been there at the temple? The age would have been appropriate for Joseph to be an older man twenty-one years later. If Joseph was there, how did this early experience with Jesus affect his generous offer to bury Jesus in his family tomb years later?

YOUR THOUGHTS

After the Bible Story

YOUR MEDITATION CAN continue after the finding of Jesus in the temple is over.

- Perhaps Jesus talked excitedly to his parents about the event, as children will: "This happened, and then that happened, and I saw this, and I saw that. And the *best* part was ..." Imagine what he said.
- Jesus said that he stayed back because he had to be about his father's business. Luke writes that his parents didn't really understand that comment. You can pretend that you are Mary or Joseph as they try to decide what Jesus meant and what to feel about it.

YOUR THOUGHTS

_____

_____

_____

_____

_____

_____

_____

A Samaritan Woman Getting Water

<hr />

IN THE GOSPEL of John (4:1–42), Jesus sees and deliberately approaches a Samaritan woman who is drawing water from a well at midday.

There are three problems here, and they all give you opportunities for meditating and pondering:

- First, good Jewish men did not talk to women outside their families.
- Second, reputable women did not have to separate themselves from other women by going for water at off hours—that is, in the heat of the sun. This woman must have had a reputation that made the other women avoid her.
- Third, from the point of view of the Jews at the time of Jesus, Samaritans were little better than animals. You certainly didn't go out of your way to talk to one, especially a woman.

But Jesus did. He deliberately approached her, carried on a lengthy conversation with her, and even made her the first person to whom he admitted that he was the Messiah.

The Woman's Point of View

———————⚬———————

WHAT DID THE woman think and feel?

She knew that he was Jewish and that he (presumably) hated her. Perhaps she was prejudiced against him too. The ancestral hatred, after all, worked both ways. What went through her mind?

- Did she wonder what kind of crazy man he had to be to go against the rules so blatantly?
- Did she expect him to suggest—or even force—a sexual encounter? He could easily rape her, out in the middle of nowhere.
- Would he kill her? Stranger things had happened.
- Or could he actually be the Messiah?
- If he was, what did it mean that he approached the likes of her? Maybe God actually could love her. What a thought!

YOUR THOUGHTS

_____

_____

_____

_____

_____

_____

The Disciples' Point of View

WHAT DID THE disciples think and feel when they eventually came upon the scene and saw the interplay between Jesus and the woman?

John says that none of them asked him certain questions. You can bet that they wanted to, and they kept their mouths shut with some difficulty:

- Were the disciples shocked? Or had they grown used to the idea that Jesus usually did the unexpected?
- Were they annoyed at having to be prepared for almost anything from him? Were they just confused—again? They spent a lot of time being confused.
- What was their interpretation of what Jesus was doing? Could some of them actually have understood?

YOUR THOUGHTS

_____
_____
_____
_____
_____
_____
_____

In Peter's Mind

PETER IS A very interesting man. He's impulsive, loyal, loud-mouthed, strong, scared, weak, faithful, and much more. He's human.

Imagine a time that is shortly after the transfiguration. In the past few days, then, Jesus has

- praised Peter lovingly by calling him the rock on which the church will be built (Matthew 16:16 and others),
- chastised Peter painfully by calling him Satan (Mark 16:23 and others), and
- honored Peter by inviting him to witness the transfiguration (Matthew 17:1–9 and others).

In short, for Peter, it has been an emotional roller coaster.

Imagine, now, that Peter is tired, at the end of a string of very hard days. He is thinking about this roller-coaster ride with Christ. Think with him.

- Does Peter yearn for earlier days that were easier, less confusing, less frightening, and less dangerous than now? Or when he thinks about those days, does he shake his head and smile over his own earlier naïveté?
- Does he remember specific moments of clarity and growth along his path to where he is now? Which ones stand out for him?

- Does he recall specific moments of failures and foibles along the same path? What did he learn from them? For example, does he now know why Jesus called him Satan?
- When he thinks about the road ahead, does he really believe that Jesus will die?
- How much is he beginning to understand about what his own mission will be?

Your Thoughts

_____

_____

_____

_____

_____

_____

_____

A Young Boy in the Crowd

ONE DAY, WHEN Jesus is teaching, perhaps one of the listeners has brought his toddler son along to hear him. We know that children sometimes discern realities that adults do not. What is this child thinking?

- Could the child know, somehow, that this dusty preacher with the achy feet is really God?
- Were they looking at each other intently during the talk?
- Is this boy one of the children that Jesus touched when he said that the children should not be hindered from approaching him?
- What might the child be thinking, a couple of years later, when the nice man is crucified?
- Who and what might the little boy have grown up to be? Could he have become one of the first martyrs?

YOUR THOUGHTS

_____

_____

_____

_____

_____

_____

Outside Actual Bible Stories

———

THERE IS NO way that any of us know how God feels and thinks. Still, he did make us in his image, and we are allowed to imagine his thoughts and feelings.

Doing so is a type of prayer, another way of getting close to him.

GOD MAKING A NEW SOUL

In this scenario, God is getting ready to make a new soul. Perhaps the scene is some years ago, and the soul will be yours.

The Bible often describes God as a potter, but he can be any kind of creator you want to imagine: a jeweler, a painter, a carpenter.

In this endeavor, God is both excited and careful. He is already half in love with the creature he's going to make. It will be one of a kind—a potential masterpiece.

Watch him choose the materials to use, selecting some and rejecting others. Why does he reject one thing that is beautiful? Why does he select another that seems plain?

Listen to him express his hopes for this creature, knowing that he cannot interfere with its free will. Perhaps you can even talk with him about the selections he makes while creating you.

- Why does he add a particular piece that will feel like a flaw or a frustration in your nature? Is it supposed to serve as raw material for you to build something yourself?

- Why does he leave out a feature or quality that you wish was part of your nature? Is its absence indeed a flaw? If so, can you use that fact to teach, guide, or support your neighbor?
- In the creation that is you, are there many dark colors mixed in with the ones that are glittery and bright? How might God, like other artists, mix the dark and the bright to create complex beauty?

Your Thoughts

_____

_____

_____

_____

_____

_____

_____

The Specter of Damnation

IN THIS SCENARIO, God sees that one of his children isn't using his free will in the best of ways. In fact, God is facing the likelihood that his creation is going to be damned.

Matthew 18:14 notes, "It is not the will of your Father which is in heaven, that one of these little ones should perish" (King James Version). Therefore, God tries to help his child, although he will not take away free will.

- When God sees his child not praying, not listening, not even believing, how does he try to get that child's attention? Do his methods change over time as the child continues to ignore God's efforts?

- Think about how you would feel if you saw your child reaching for a can of lye. Could God feel a bit like that when he sees his child reaching for sin?

- God's commandments are precious to him; that's why he spoke them so often and so intensely. God sees his lost child breaking yet another commandment. Think how you might feel if you saw someone you loved deliberately destroying something you prized, right in front of your eyes.

And when it's obvious that the person's choices will not improve and that his or her fate will indeed be damnation, what

might God think and feel then? What might he say to his lost
child or to himself?

Your Thoughts

_____

_____

_____

_____

_____

_____

_____

In Conclusion: A Fine Addiction

THE TYPE OF meditation that has been demonstrated, described, and encouraged in this book involves asking questions, carrying on mental conversations, and empathizing with the deepest thoughts and feelings of people in the Bible and even of God.

It reminds you that you do not need to be a great saint to meditate. And it invites you to take your raw material from the small events, feelings, and people, rather than, necessarily, from the vast, holy, and famous ones.

This kind of thinking can be addictive, but it is a fine addiction. If you let it, it can even lead you out from under your own bushel.

Printed in the United States
By Bookmasters